SHADOW-WORK
JOURNAL

🔓 **Discover Your Hidden Self & Unleash Your True Potential!**

The
SHADOW WORK
JOURNAL

THIS JOURNAL BELONGS TO:

_____

_____

_____

Declaration of Intent

I, _____, consciously declare my genuine intent to embark on this journey of self-discovery and transformation. With this declaration, I commit to:

Honesty: I will remain truthful, even when faced with the most challenging truths about myself, embracing both my light and shadow.

Open-mindedness: I will approach this journey with a receptive heart and mind, ready to explore unfamiliar terrains and challenge long-held beliefs.

Dedication: I understand that meaningful change requires time and consistent effort. I am prepared to invest both, fully committing to this path.

Self-compassion: Recognizing that introspection might unearth vulnerabilities, I promise to be gentle with myself, approaching each revelation with kindness and understanding.

Learning: I am eager to grow, evolve, and expand my horizons. I am open to lessons, whether they come as affirmations or challenges.

Respect for the Process: I will honor each stage of this journey, understanding that every step, no matter how minor, contributes to my overall growth.

With this declaration, I set forth my intention, shaping my journey towards self-awareness, healing, and transformation. I trust in the process and embrace the adventure that lies ahead with courage and determination.

_____   _____   _____

Signature]   [Start Date]   [Completion Date]

SHADOW WORK

What do you know about shadow work?

ne concept of "shadow work" is centered around
e "shadow self". It is the part of ourselves that we
e as dark and diabolic. It is the demon inside of
. We often feel ashamed, insecure, or even
ustrated about this shadow self of ours. Therefore,
e try to push it away by burying it inside.

ne notion of "shadow self" is firstly presented by
wiss psychologist **"Carl Jung"** after he spent
ears of human personality studying.
he shadow self manifests in many ways under
any circumstances. For instance, we see its
anifestation clearly when we feel intrigued by
her people's actions or words.

Afterward, this shadow self is represented in so many ways and different names. It is our Dark Passenger according to Dexter. Or Mr. Hyde according to R.L. Stevenson.

Most of the time, we push this shadow self far away from us, keep it in a tiny box and lock it, until we even no longer remember what's in it! We no longer know our dark selves. This unhealthy situation makes us in a state of dishonesty with ourselves until it takes us to a state of hypocrisy and self-distraction.

This is what shadow work is about, it helps you be open with yourself, know yourself better, reconcile with your dark self instead of burying it, and consequently control it.

This journal contains many prompts to help you practice shadow work, by appealing to different situations from your past or present days. Please be honest and open to yourself.

SHADOW WORK

How to Do Shadow Work?

When Carl Jung, the revered Swiss psychiatrist, first introduced the concept of the "shadow self," little did he know that he was unveiling a powerful tool for deep introspection and self-growth.

At the heart of Jung's philosophy is a simple yet profound idea: each of us carries a dark side, an unconscious part made up of desires, fears, and experiences we'd rather not acknowledge. This is our "shadow." But, contrary to what many think, shadow work isn't about banishing this darkness; it's about embracing, understanding, and integrating it.

SHADOW WORK

Why Should You Consider Shadow Work?

Before delving deep into the intricacies of the 'how,' it's crucial to pause and reflect upon the compelling reasons or the 'why' behind this journey. The essence of the matter is stark: when we choose to turn a blind eye or consciously suppress the aspects of our shadow self, we inadvertently pave the way for a tumultuous storm of emotional disturbances.

This neglect can manifest in various ways, including relationships that constantly seem to crumble, patterns of self-destruction, and a life that feels disjointed from who we truly are at our core. On the flip side, when we muster the courage to embrace and understand this shadow, the rewards are transformative. We open doors to a heightened level of self-awareness, foster healthier and more genuine relationships, and set ourselves on a path of profound personal evolution and growth.

SHADOW WORK

Step-by-Step Guide to Doing Shadow Work

1. Introspection and Acknowledgment:
Start by creating a quiet, introspective space. Through meditation or simple stillness, allow thoughts and feelings to arise. Instead of judging or pushing them away, acknowledge them. This is the first step in recognizing your shadow.

2. Journaling:
Write down these feelings, thoughts, or memories that you might usually suppress. Journaling is a powerful tool in shadow work because it provides clarity, allowing you to confront your thoughts without judgment.

3. Seek Triggers:

Notice what triggers negative reactions in you. Often, what we vehemently oppose in others is a reflection of our shadow. These triggers can act as signposts pointing towards what lies in our unconscious.

4. Practice Compassion:

Understand that everyone has a shadow, molded by experiences, upbringing, and society. Practicing self-compassion is crucial. Be gentle with yourself; this work isn't about self-blame but about understanding and integration.

5. Engage in Dialogue with Your Shadow:

Yes, this might sound peculiar, but having a 'conversation' with your shadow can be enlightening. Ask it questions: "Why do you make me feel this way?" or "What are you trying to show me?" Listen to its answers.

6. Seek Professional Guidance:

A therapist or counselor trained in Jungian techniques or shadow work can provide invaluable insights and tools to guide you through this journey.

7. Use Creative Outlets:

Art, dance, music, or any form of creativity can be therapeutic and a means of expressing and understanding the shadow.

SHADOW WORK

Benefits of Embracing Your Shadow

Holistic Self-Awareness: Get to know your complete self, not just the parts you show to the world.

Improved Relationships: By understanding your triggers and reactions, you can communicate better and relate more authentically to others.

Personal Growth: Breaking free from self-imposed limitations and realizing your true potential.

Enhanced Creativity: When you integrate all parts of yourself, including the suppressed emotions and desires, you'll find they can fuel your creativity in unparalleled ways.

In a world that often champions relentless positivity, the idea of diving deep into our darker parts might seem counterintuitive. But therein lies the beauty of shadow work. It's not about focusing on the negative; it's about acknowledging that light and dark, together, create a complete, authentic picture.

When you start this journey, remember: the goal isn't to 'fix' or 'banish' the shadow. It's to understand, embrace, and integrate it. Because only by facing our darkness can we truly step into our light.

So, will you take the brave step towards a more authentic, integrated self? The transformative power of shadow work awaits in this book.

SHADOW WORK

How to Use This Book

Navigating the depths of your inner self migh
seem daunting, but with the right tools, th
journey becomes a transformative experienc
This book is one such tool, tailored for you
introspective expedition. With prompts crafte
under the careful guidance of experience
therapists, you are in safe hands.

**Here's your roadmap to harnessing th
book's full potential:**

Cultivate A Safe Space:
Begin by identifying a quiet, serene space wher
you can reflect without interruptions. Thi
sanctuary will set the tone for dee
introspection.

Pledge Honesty:
The heart of shadow work is raw, unfiltered truth. Approach each prompt with a commitment to total honesty, even when it feels uncomfortable.

Pace Yourself:
Do not feel pressured to rush through the prompts. Some may evoke powerful reactions; it's okay to take breaks, process, and then return.

Document Your Insights:
As you work through the prompts, jot down your reflections. This act not only deepens the process but also serves as a record of your journey.

Re-Engagement:
Our inner landscapes change. Consider revisiting the prompts periodically to gauge your growth and delve deeper into different layers of your psyche.

Trust In The Therapeutic Foundation:
Rest assured, every prompt in this book has a therapeutic basis. They are designed to guide, challenge, and help you unfold.

Reach Out When Necessary:
Digging deep can occasionally feel overwhelming. If emotions become too intense, remember it's okay to seek additional support from professionals.

By immersing yourself wholeheartedly in this book, you're not only exploring your shadow self but also nurturing personal growth. Here's to your brave voyage into the depths of self-awareness and transformation.

YOUR PARENTS

Did your parents provide you with everything you wanted or needed?

CHILDHOOD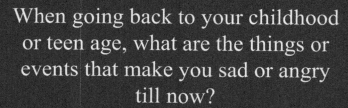

When going back to your childhood
or teen age, what are the things or
events that make you sad or angry
till now?

CHILDHOOD

Why do these childhood or teenage flashbacks of yours make you so angry or sad?

CHILDHOOD

Have you ever been assaulted or harassed as a child or a teenager? How does it make you feel when you think about it?

CHILDHOOD

Will you describe your childhood as happy? Why?

HURTNESS

If you are able to write a letter
to every person who hurt you
somehow, what would it be?

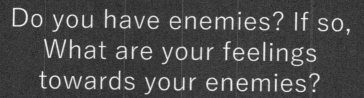

ENEMIES

Do you have enemies? If so,
What are your feelings
towards your enemies?

FORGIVENESS

Do you find it hard to forgive? and how much does it take for you to forgive?

FORGIVENESS

Do you think you can forgive
people who hurt you? Why?

TRUST

Do you trust people or do you have issues with trust?

RELATIONSHIPS

What friendships or relationships do you hold onto that you think are unhealthy? Why?

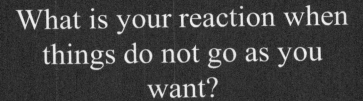

YOUR REACTION

What is your reaction when things do not go as you want?

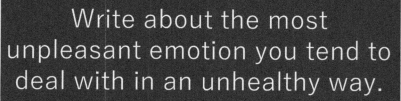

EMOTIONS

Write about the most unpleasant emotion you tend to deal with in an unhealthy way.

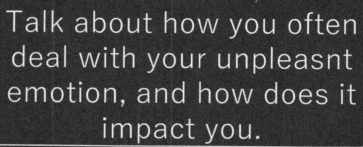

EMOTIONS

Talk about how you often deal with your unpleasnt emotion, and how does it impact you.

FRANKNESS

Are you always honest with others about your feelings?

HEALTHY

Try to find five ways to deal with your hard feelings in a healthy way

THE PRESENT

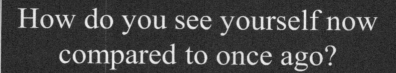

How do you see yourself now
compared to once ago?

SELF NEGATIVES

To what degree do you think you are hypocritical? How often do you break your own rules or principles? Do you often hold people to a higher standard than you hold yourself?

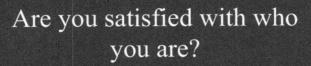

SATISFICTION

Are you satisfied with who
you are?

SATISFICTION

Are you always honest with
yourself about your feelings?

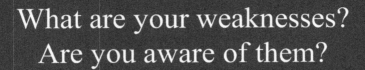

SATISFICTION

What are your weaknesses?
Are you aware of them?

SADNESS

What makes you feel the saddest?

HAPPINESS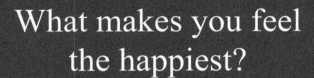

What makes you feel the happiest?

CONFIDENCE

Do you trust yourself?

PERSONALITY

What situations or events have
shaped my personality, and
made me who I am?

FAILURE

How do you deal with failure?
Do you blame yourself or
others?

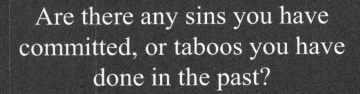

RECOGNITION

Are there any sins you have committed, or taboos you have done in the past?

RECOGNITION

What do you feel when
thinking about these taboos and
sins...pleasure or regret? Why?

If you are to write a letter to the old you, what would you say?

What fatal mistakes you have
made that you think had a
changing impact on your life?

WHILE SLEEPING

Are you having dreams or nightmares? How do you feel about them, and What do you think they mean?

FANTASM

Do you have some personal and secret fetishes, dark desires, fantasies...?!

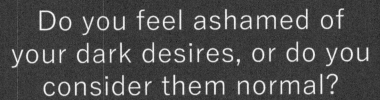

DARK DESIRES

Do you feel ashamed of
your dark desires, or do you
consider them normal?

Let's Talk About Dark Passenger

he Dark Passenger is a notion or a concept that presents our dark self, the demon inside of us, at affects us and urges us to commit evil eeds. In the T.V show "DEXTER", this dark assenger concept is well presented.

very one of us has a Dark Passenger of his own. is important to become aware of yours, and now how to deal with it. If you give in, you are longer in charge, you are no longer driving ehind your actions...your Dark Passenger does hat it wants until you are broken and evastated.

DARK PASSENGER

When did you become aware of your Dark Passenger?

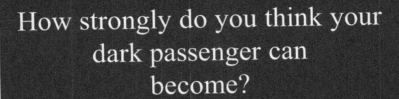

DARK PASSENGER

How strongly do you think your dark passenger can become?

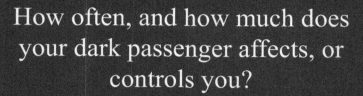

DARK PASSENGER

How often, and how much does your dark passenger affects, or controls you?

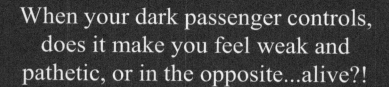

DARK PASSENGER

When your dark passenger controls, does it make you feel weak and pathetic, or in the opposite...alive?!

DARK PASSENGER

Do you fight your Dark Passenger
and resist him, or...you don't want
to ?!!!

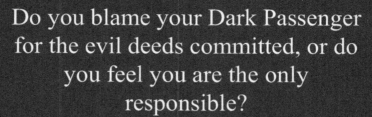

DARK PASSENGER

Do you blame your Dark Passenger for the evil deeds committed, or do you feel you are the only responsible?

Free Space
FOR PERSONAL NOTES

In case you want to talk about Other
things....

Free Space
FOR PERSONAL NOTES

Free Space
FOR PERSONAL NOTES

Free Space
FOR PERSONAL NOTES

Free Space
FOR PERSONAL NOTES

Free Space
FOR PERSONAL NOTES

Free Space
FOR PERSONAL NOTES

Free Space
FOR PERSONAL NOTES

Free Space
FOR PERSONAL NOTES

Free Space
FOR PERSONAL NOTES

Free Space
FOR PERSONAL NOTES

Free Space
FOR PERSONAL NOTES

Free Space
FOR PERSONAL NOTES

Made in the USA
Las Vegas, NV
26 September 2023

78132852R00063